DOGS, PUPPIES & DOGS!

A FUN ACTIVITY BOOK FOR ALL AGES

Hello!

Welcome to this super amazing book and thank you for purchasing (or, if it's a gift and you're the recipient – thanks for reading!). You'll also soon be sketching, searching and solving, because this book is virtually brimming with fun activities to complete, all with a canine theme.

So grab yourself:

A ballpoint

A pencil

A rubber

A ruler

A pair of eyes (preferably your own)

...and let's begin!

ANSWERS TO PUZZLES CAN BE FOUND AT THE END OF THE BOOK!

YOUR NAME

_____

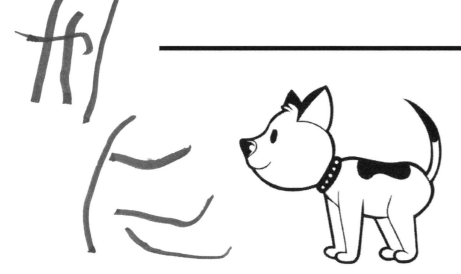

YOUR NAME IF YOU WERE A DOG?

_____

SPOT THE DOG!

ONLY ONE DOG IS UNIQUE. BUT WHICH?

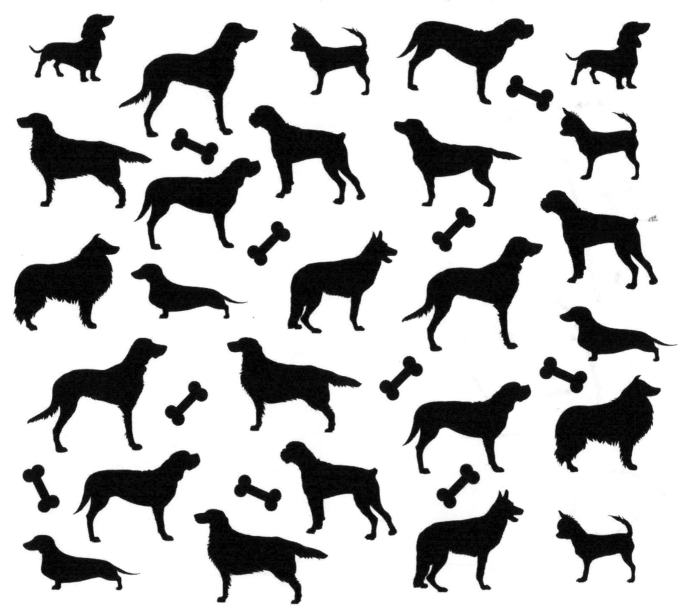

DOG BREEDS

B _ S _ E _ _ _ _ _ D

_ E _ I _ G _ S _

_ O O _ _ _

B _ _ LM _ _ TI _ _

S _ _ _ L _ _ D S _ _ _ P _ _ G

L _ B _ _ D _ R

SI _ _ _ I _ N _ U _ K _

SPOT THE DIFFERENCE!

See if you can locate all five differences

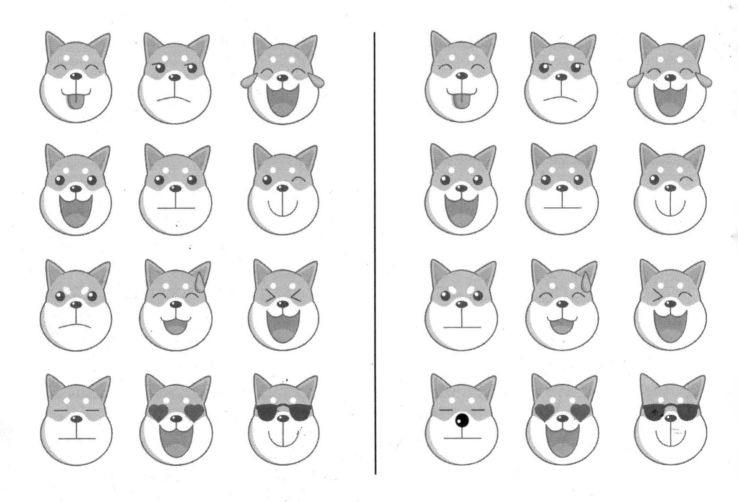

Mirror Mutts

Mirror Mutts

BAD DOG!

A DOG'S BEEN CAUGHT STEALING A BONE.
CAN YOU IDENTIFY THE PAW PRINT LOCATED
AT THE SCENE OF THE CRIME?

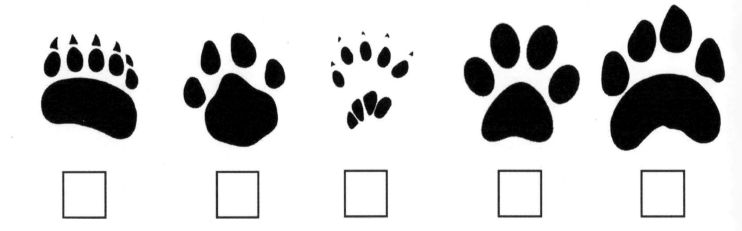

DINNER TIME!

HELP THE DOG FIND ITS FOOD

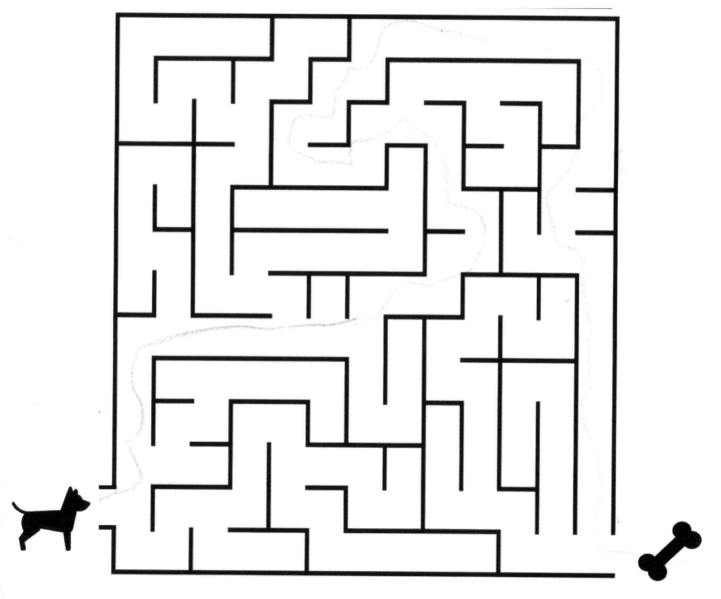

DOGGY DUPLICATES!

ALL THE DOGS ARE DUPLICATES EXCEPT TWO. BUT WHICH?

SO MANY DOG BREEDS!

U	N	L	F	B	I	R	E	R	C	H	E	S	C
D	C	L	I	L	L	E	S	E	R	S	O	D
H	S	A	A	T	G	I	U	I	R	T	R	E	A
D	A	L	M	A	T	I	A	N	F	G	T	T	C
L	L	T	E	R	R	I	E	R	I	T	B	E	H
T	H	B	I	C	H	I	H	U	A	H	U	A	S
B	H	L	B	U	L	A	F	H	D	B	I	R	H
U	A	E	O	X	O	R	C	F	R	N	I	A	U
L	R	H	X	R	E	C	O	D	I	N	U	T	N
L	P	F	E	W	L	O	L	S	E	T	E	O	D
D	D	U	R	A	H	D	L	O	W	O	S	I	H
O	R	O	T	T	W	E	I	L	E	R	D	A	T
G	P	I	N	S	C	H	E	R	C	E	R	G	M
I	S	O	A	B	L	S	E	E	I	R	A	H	R

CHIHUAHUA

BULLDOG

TERRIER

COLLIE

BOXER

HOUND

BEAGLE

CORGI

ROTTWEILER

PINSCHER

DALMATIAN

SETTER

MASTIFF

DACHSHUND

BONES VS PAW PRINTS
Who has the most?

TWIN-SPOTTING

MANY ARE TRIPLETS BUT ONLY ONE PAIR ARE TWINS.
CAN YOU FIND WHICH?

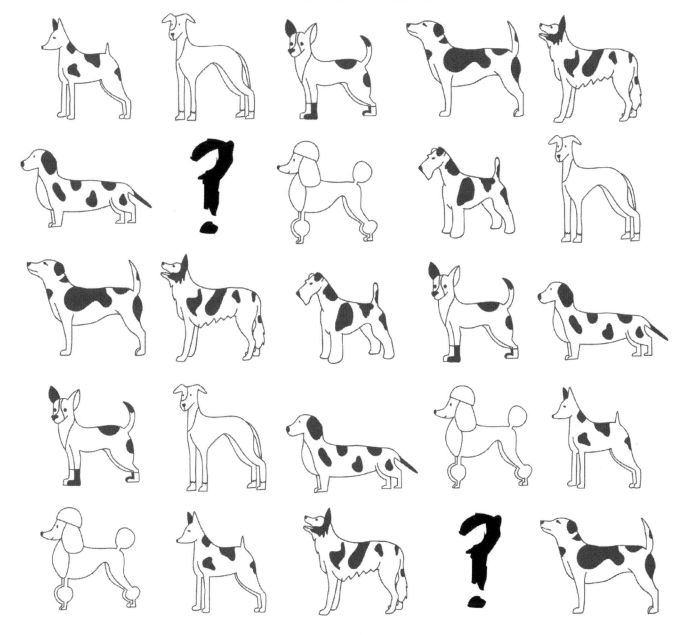

WHERE'S THE DOG?

D G G O O D O D G G O G D O
G D O D O G G O G G O G D O
O G O O G G O G G O O D G O
G D O O D O O O G O O D G
G O G O D G O O G O G D D O
G D O D D O D G O G D O D G
O D G D O D O G O O D O D G

COPY THE CANINES!

See if you can give the dogs an identical twin!

DOG BREEDS

G _ E _ _ D _ N _

_ _ T T _ E _ L _ R

_ U _ L _ _ G

_ H _ H _ A _ U _

D _ _ _ _ _ _ _ D

E _ _ L I _ _ M _ _ T _ F _

B _ _ D _ R _ O _ _ _ E

Name Calling

A PAGE FOR ALL YOUR FAVOURITE DOGGY NAMES. YOU CAN COME BACK TO THIS
WHEN YOU GET A NEW POOCH!

SPOT THE DOGS

THREE DOGS ARE UNIQUE... BUT WHICH?

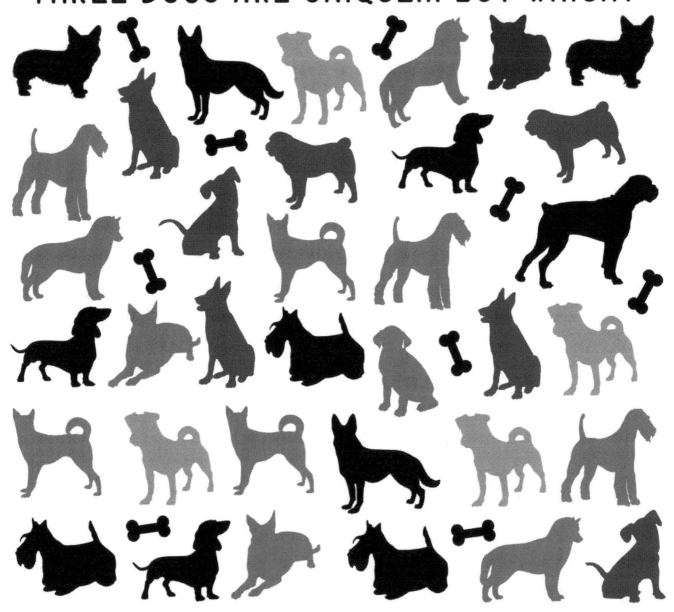

GUESS THE BREED!

Things I Love About Dogs...

THE ROAD TO FOOD
ONLY ONE ROAD LEADS TO THE BOWL!

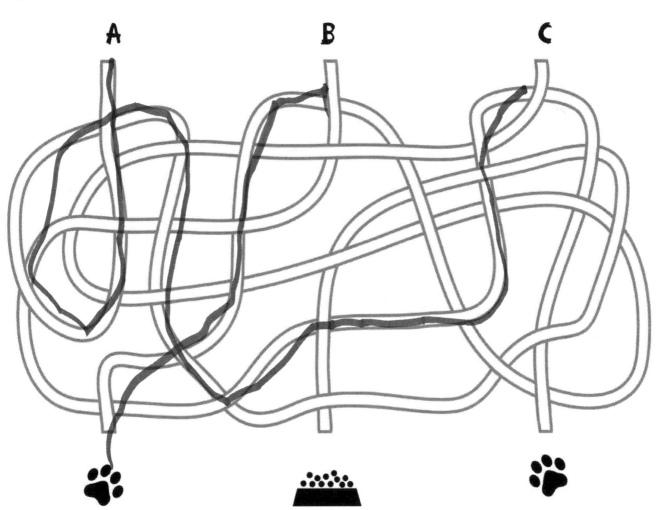

DESIGN YOUR DREAM
DOG RELATED JUMPER!

MORE DOG BREEDS!

B	B	I	B	L	O	O	D	H	O	U	N	D	I
I	A	B	O	R	D	E	R	C	O	L	L	I	E
F	S	R	B	R	O	D	A	R	B	A	L	T	R
R	S	E	O	L	N	S	B	I	D	O	I	U	E
F	E	T	X	D	R	O	B	O	A	E	O	H	H
O	T	R	E	T	O	Z	I	R	R	E	L	O	C
X	H	I	R	F	S	R	H	I	D	Z	X	I	R
H	O	E	H	O	S	N	N	A	I	I	O	R	U
O	U	V	E	I	R	E	T	N	I	O	P	I	L
U	N	E	I	R	I	S	H	S	E	T	T	E	R
N	D	R	F	F	I	T	S	A	M	L	L	U	B
D	I	F	Z	D	A	L	S	A	T	I	A	N	N
A	F	F	E	N	P	I	N	S	C	H	E	R	R
O	I	P	R	E	F	S	B	O	E	T	N	V	O

ALSATIAN
LABRADOR
RETRIEVER
AFFENPINSCHER
BASSET HOUND
BLOODHOUND
BORDER COLLIE
BORZOI
BOXER
BULLMASTIFF
FOXHOUND
IRISH SETTER
POINTER
LURCHER

DOGGY DUPLICATES!

ALL THE DOGS ARE DUPLICATES EXCEPT THREE. BUT WHICH?

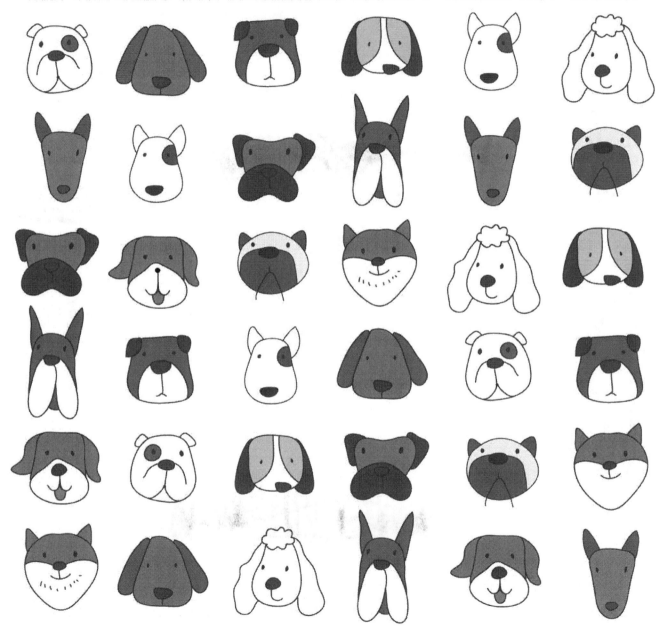

SPOT THE DOG! WHICH DOG IS UNIQUE?

Four words to sum up a Dog

DOGGY DOODLES! COLOUR ME IN!

DOG BREEDS

G _ E _ _ D _ N _

_ _ T T _ E _ L _ R

_ U _ L _ _ G

_ H _ H _ A _ U _

D _ _ _ _ _ _ _ D

E _ _ L I _ _ M _ _ T _ F _

B _ _ D _ R _ O _ _ _ E

DOGGY DUPLICATES!
ALL THE DOGS ARE DUPLICATES EXCEPT TWO. BUT WHICH?

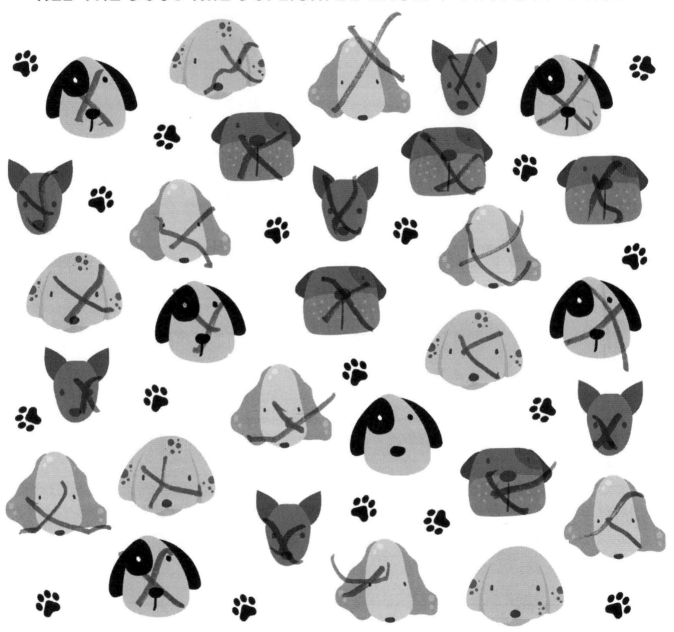

DOGS BODY!
CAN YOU DRAW ONE FOR THIS CUTE PUG?

TOTAL NUMBER OF JACK RUSSELLS

32

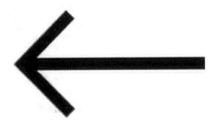

Mirror Mutts

DOGGY DOUBLES!

THERE ARE THREE SET OF TWINS HIDING HERE. CAN YOU SPOT THEM?

:: COLOUR MY DOGS! ::

Match the Breed!

Beagle   Ibizan Hound   Schnauzer

Pinscher   Bulldog   Shiba Inu

A DOGS TAIL!

CAN YOU FIND THE **TWO DOGS** WITH **MISSING TAILS?**

COPY THE CANINES!

See if you can give the dogs an identical twin!

DOG BREEDS

C _ O _   C _ _ _

Y _ R _ _ _ _ R _   _ E _ _ I _ R

_ H _ H   T _ _

G _ E _ _ O _ _ D

_ O _ D _ N   _ E _ R _ E _ E _

G _ _ _ A N   S _ _ P _ _ _ D

S _   _ _ R N _ _ D

COLOUR ME!

GUESS THE BREED!

SKETCH ME

ANOTHER LOST DOG!

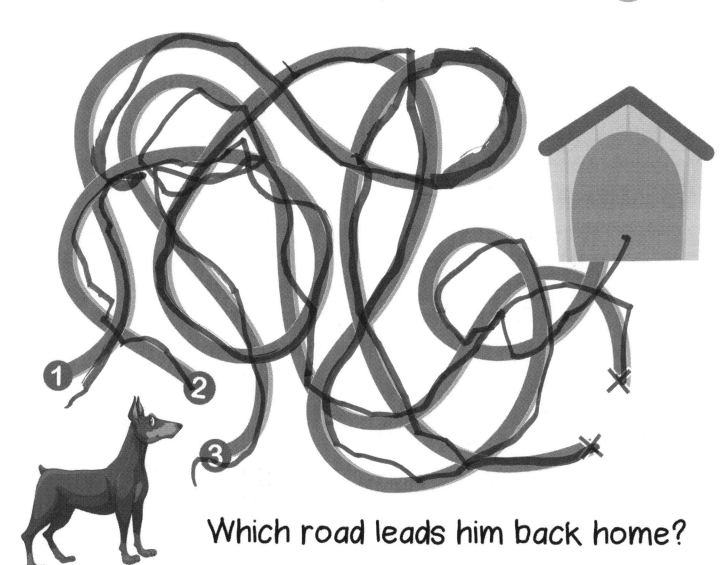

Which road leads him back home?

MATCH THE BREED!

GOLDEN RETRIEVER   SIBERIAN WOLF   BULL TERRIER

GERMAN SHEPHERD   BULLDOG   POMERANIA

SPOT THE DOGGY DIFFERENCES!

CAN YOU SPOT THE 4 DIFFERENCES?

AWWW!
DOGS AND PUPPIES IN LOVE!

SPOT THE DOG
ONLY ONE DOG IS UNIQUE. BUT WHICH?

WHICH ANIMAL GETS TO MEET A DOG?

MATCH THE BREED!

PITBULL   SCHNAUZER   DALMATION

CHIHUAHUA   POODLE   COCKER SPANIEL

ANSWERS

SPOT THE DOG!
ONLY ONE DOG IS UNIQUE. BUT WHICH?

DINNER TIME!

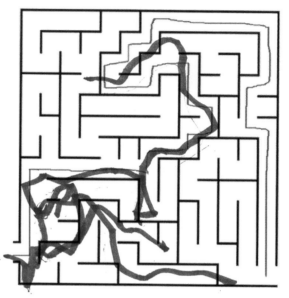

SPOT THE DIFFERENCE!
See if you can locate all five differences

DOGGY DUPLICATES!
ALL THE DOGS ARE DUPLICATES EXCEPT TWO. BUT WHICH?

DOG BREED MISSING LETTERS

GREAT DANE
ROTTWEILER
BULLDOG
CHIHUAHUA
DACHSHUND
ENGLISH MASTIFF
BORDER COLLIE

CHOW CHOW
YORKSHIRE TERRIER
SHIH TZU
GREYHOUND
GOLDEN RETRIEVER
GERMAN SHEPHERD
ST BERNARD

BASSET HOUND
PEKINGESE
POODLE
BULLMASTIFF
SHETLAND SHEEPDOG
LABRADOR
SIBERIAN HUSKY

TOTAL NUMBER
OF JACK
RUSSELLS
32

There are **23** Paw Prints and **24** Bones
Bones win!

A DOG'S BEEN CAUGHT STEALING A BONE. CAN YOU IDENTIFY THE PAW PRINT LOCATED AT THE SCENE OF THE CRIME?

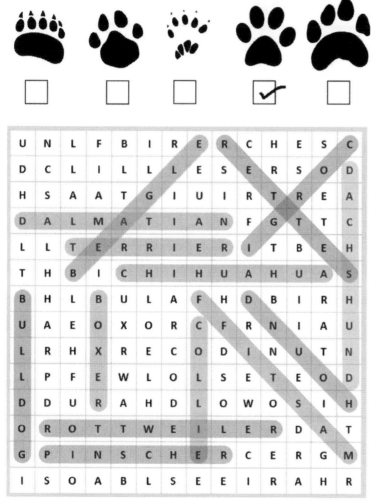

THE ROAD TO FOOD:
CORRECT ANSWER
C

TWIN-SPOTTING
MANY ARE TRIPLETS BUT ONLY ONE PAIR ARE TWINS.
CAN YOU FIND WHICH?

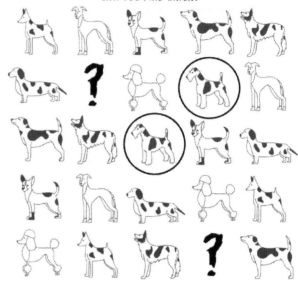

WHERE'S THE DOG?

D G G O O D O D G G O G D O
G D O D O G G O G G O G D O
O G O O G G O G G O O D G O
G D O O D O O G O O O D G
G O G O D G O O G O O D D O
G D O D D D O G O G D O D G
O D G D O D O G O O D O R G

SPOT THE DOGS

THREE DOGS ARE UNIQUE... BUT WHICH?

DOGGY DUPLICATES!

ALL THE DOGS ARE DUPLICATES EXCEPT THREE. BUT WHICH?

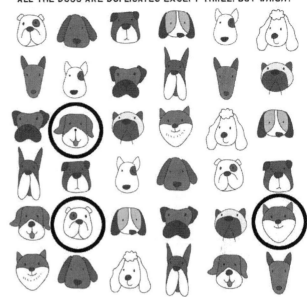

- FRENCH BULLDOG -
- ROTTWEILER -
- CHIHUAHUA -
- SIBERIAN HUSKY -
- SCHNAUZER -
- DACHSHUND -

B	B	I	B	L	O	O	D	H	O	U	N	D	I
I	A	B	O	R	D	E	R	C	O	L	L	I	E
F	S	R	B	R	O	D	A	R	B	A	L	T	R
R	S	E	O	L	N	S	B	I	D	O	I	U	E
F	E	T	X	D	R	O	B	O	A	E	O	H	H
O	T	R	E	T	O	Z	I	R	R	E	L	O	C
X	H	I	R	F	S	R	H	I	D	Z	X	I	R
H	O	E	H	O	S	N	N	A	I	I	O	R	U
O	U	V	E	I	R	E	T	N	I	O	P	I	L
U	N	E	I	R	I	S	H	S	E	T	T	E	R
N	D	R	F	F	I	T	S	A	M	L	L	U	B
D	I	F	Z	D	A	L	S	A	T	I	A	N	N
A	F	F	E	N	P	I	N	S	C	H	E	R	R
O	I	P	R	E	F	S	B	O	E	T	N	V	O

SPOT THE DOG! WHICH DOG IS UNIQUE?

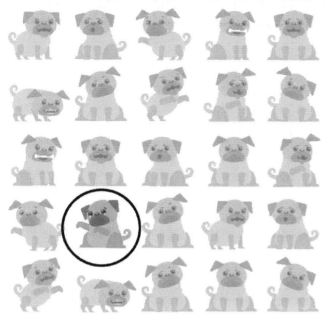

DOGGY DUPLICATES!
ALL THE DOGS ARE DUPLICATES EXCEPT TWO. BUT WHICH?

THE LOST DOG

START

END

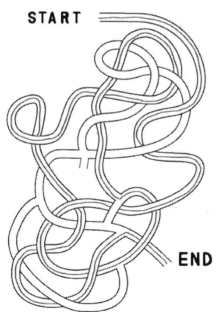

DOGGY DOUBLES!
THERE ARE THREE SET OF TWINS HIDING HERE. CAN YOU SPOT THEM?

Schnauzer

Ibizan Hound

Shiba Inu

Beagle

Pinscher

Bulldog

A DOGS **TAIL!**

CAN YOU FIND THE **TWO DOGS** WITH **MISSING TAILS?**

(o LABRADOR RETRIEVER o)

(o BULLDOG o)

(o YORKSHIRE TERRIER o)

(o BEAGLE o)

(o POODLE o)

(o BOXER o)

SPOT THE DOGGY DIFFERENCE!

CAN YOU SPOT THE 4 DIFFERENCES?

MATCH THE BREED!

BULLDOG

POMERANIA

SIBERIAN
WOLF

BULL
TERRIER

GERMAN
SHEPHERD

GOLDEN
RETRIVER

MATCH THE BREED!

DALMATION

CHIHUAHUA

POODLE

PITBULL

SCHNAUZER

COCKER SPANIEL

ANOTHER LOST DOG! = 2

SPOT THE DOG
ONLY ONE DOG IS UNIQUE. BUT WHICH?

WHICH ANIMAL GETS TO MEET A DOG?

THE LEOPARD!

COUNT THE PAWS
= 73

THE END!

OTHER ACTIVITY BOOKS ALSO AVAILABLE!

CATS, KITTENS AND CATS!

BIRDS, OWLS AND BIRDS!

BUGS, SPIDERS AND INSECTS!

FISH, DOLPHINS AND FISH!

ANIMALS IN THE WILD!

ANIMALS ON THE FARM!

HAPPY HALLOWEEN!

MERRY CHRISTMAS!

SUPERHEROES!

MONSTERS!

Made in the USA
Middletown, DE
06 September 2019